Love is . . .

By Dr. Michelle Butler

Illustrated by Michele Presley

Vabella Publishing
P.O. Box 1052
Carrollton, Georgia 30112
www.vabella.com

©Copyright 2024 Michelle Butler

All rights reserved. No part of the book may be reproduced or utilized in any form or by any means without permission in writing from the author. All requests should be addressed to the publisher.

Manufactured in the United States of America

ISBN 979-8-89450-015-7

Patient

You can do it!

Kind

Not envious

Not boastful

Not proud

I'm sorry.

Not delighting in evil

Always protective

Always trusting

Can you take care of my snail?

Always hopeful

I can do it!

Always persevering

Not self-seeking

Not easily angered

You can have mine.

Not dishonoring others

We shouldn't talk badly about him.

Keeping no record of wrongs

Rejoicing in truth

I was saying bad things about you.

Love never fails

Faith, love, and hope

That is what love is all about

About the Author

Dr. Michelle Butler resides in Georgia with her husband and one of her children. You can often find her other two children dropping by to visit. Her grandchildren, who affectionately call her Mimi, are constantly present, bringing joy and energy to her home. Her door is always open to family and friends, so she creates a home where everyone feels welcome.

About the Illustrator

Michele Presley is a senior at Central High School in Carrollton, Georgia. She has a strong passion for illustration, and, in January of 2024, she wrote and illustrated her first children's book, *Winnie Whitlock's Guide to Poetry*. After high school, she plans to attend college and pursue a career in illustration.

www.ingramcontent.com/pod-product-compliance
Lightning Source LLC
LaVergne TN
LVHW070940070526
838199LV00039B/726